The Book of Aaron through the Eye's of God.........

In the heart of Washington D.C., the air was thickened with anticipation as I Aaron the United States Navy Religious Objector introduces the Silver Back Gorillaz Secret Service, emphasizing remember we the people are watching we the people are the spies for Yahweh here on this Earth. We protect our children we protect their faith and beliefs of God. I was to once confined by my past but now an unyielding spirit guides me, I stand before the monumental façade of this here White House. My journey, once fraught with personal battle wounds and emotional tribulations, had led me to this pivotal moment where earthly governance met divine guidance. As whispers of wisdom flowed through my body from the Holy Spirit, I felt a peaceful assurance about my role in fulfilling a greater purpose. The corridors of power, always bustling with political strategies and legislative agendas, seemed to hush in collective acknowledgment of this unique turning point. With clarity, I relayed the whispered messages to those in authority—a fresh perspective on liberating the minds and spirits of the American people, while reinforcing the true meaning of liberty and justice. Here, amidst the decisions of

war and peace, budgets and policies, the influence of a higher moral compass began steering the dialogue. Throughout the Pentagon, military leaders gather into the shift, recognizing the call to lead not just with power but with heart-centered humanity. It was a call to action that transcended traditional strategies, asking them to remember the core values upon which the nation was founded upon. As new political visions began to take shape, inspired by my earnest connection and message, the impact of one man's faith ushered in a transformative wave, promising a future where freedom truly lived up to its name—both for the homebound veteran and every citizen alike.

As my ideas continue to ripple through the corridors of power, the book of Aaron will become a beacon of thought leadership, drawing the attention of ambassadors from around the world. The compelling nature of concepts resonates deeply within the halls of global diplomacy, prompting discussions on their potential for reshaping international relations and cooperation. The intention for this mission is for the Senate and the Congress to recognize the profound impact of this vision when I grasp the attention of the President of the United States. I Aaron Michael Finch am and will be appointed as both a leading advisor and an honorary figurehead over the United States Military. This unprecedented appointment symbolizes a strategic shift towards embracing new ideas and fostering a partnership between innovative thought leadership and military expertise.

In this influential position, I will integrate progressive policies within the military framework. I will focus extends beyond mere defense strategies, emphasizing humanitarian missions, sustainability practices, and the pursuit of peace through diplomatic engagements. The military, under my honorary guidance, embarks on an era marked by resilience and adaptability in addressing contemporary global challenges.

My residence in this dual role catalyzes a wave of inspiration among military personnel and civilians alike, encouraging a reimagining of national and global security philosophies. My leadership will than help transform traditional views, navigating the delicate balance between maintaining national security and upholding values of global cooperation, justice, and peace.

In this reshaped environment, the world watches closely, eager to see how I Aaron Michael Finch's role will influence not just the military but also the broader context of international relations. They will be asking how will Aaron's vision of unity and progress shape the United States' interactions on the world stage, and what long-term effects will this embrace of innovative leadership have on global geopolitics? These questions are at the heart of this transformative era, setting the stage for an exciting trajectory towards a more interconnected future.

We the people say enough is enough for it is time for us to go to war. While introducing the United States Military Monopoly Act we shall walk without any fear, for we will be revising the United States Constitution. We must understand Free will, mission, communication and respect is imperative when you hear and mention Project America Limited Liability Corporation, for as citizens we our all the umbrella holders of these Nations here on Earth. When we carefully observe what is taking place here in America, we will notice that our own family members are in control and running America through our military branches. We have the United States Marine Corps, Army, United States Air Force, the Coast Guard and the United States Navy. The military protects America from infiltration and stands up for the constitution here in America so that our people can be free because we are all blessed with our free-will and our government makes sure that We Stand United, but my American brothers and sisters what are we standing united about and for what? If the world is in our control, we should be putting the right efforts into making a change. I never say go against our constitution but add to the foundation of our government to set the generations free and become balanced out. The struggles that America is faced with every year creates a reason to kill all year around and for nothing. When you get a chance look at how our brothers and sisters, cousins, aunties, and uncles to our moms and dads sacrificed for the foundation of the American people and the people of this world. Look at what our grandmother and grandfather put up with to fight for their families to be free and set a guide in front of their children's feet. Let us not be mistaken each generation has strived together to better their family's life's and them-selves so that life could present an opportunity for one another for we have been founded since 1776 and it is now 2025, that is 249 years of strengthening mankind here in America. My American brothers and sisters it is time to take our intelligence and our leadership to a new level for America is the free world. Could you imagine if all religious leaders gathered, all farmers, all school systems from 1A and up and all 4-H and boy and girl scouts to all teachers, nurses, doctors, lawyers, judges, and presidents come together to strengthen the new mission here in America for Project America Incorporated would than be in effect. I am asking all motivational and Inspirational speakers to gather around the mission recruiting movie stars, athletes, and musicians to entertain this world for the New World Order will be in effect for Project America limited liability corporation. Project America is willing to understand all organizations that are so called standing in the way of the civilians here in America. We want to gather us all as one for we don't have to have all the same dreams or views about life but move in a positive direction bringing forth change to our country and the way of life because not only do resources of the land rule the nation but people on the same accord provides the resources for the resources to remain healthy for a team work makes a dream work and this will keep the American people in line with the other 6 continents to better the systems here in this world. While laying a safety net for us all a Senior Citizen Homeless Act. And a Senior Citizen Disability Homeless Act and a Veteran Homeless Act. So, no matter who is in charge, all the American Citizens will always be taken care of and will never suffer as an elderly person here in America. I recommend that the teenagers look around at life and start asking the folks how they got in the position that they are in now? What did it take for them to receive the income that they are receiving now? Ask them how well they do in school? Pay attention to everything they say and then compare the answers to everyone else's answers and see where it leads you. See we are all in life together, but it takes different elements in life to receive certain benefits. School is especially important. Make sure you do not get caught up in your friend's conversations about school not being important. Majority of good jobs you need to receive a college degree. To become an officer in the military you need a college degree, all these employments you will receive a higher salary paying job with a college degree. Meaning if you live in a bad neighborhood, you will be able to move out and remember just because you move out does not mean you will forget about the people there, the question is which side are you on? Are you on the side to help the people or entrap them inside the government? The voice of a man shall never be forgotten. As long as his actions lines up with his words. Who am I and what is it that I would like to become? As my mind veers off track delving into reality of all situations I began to understand my prize relies on me conquering my fears. What is it about the Police Department that I shall let my dreams diminish following into the hands of the devil while entrapping my vision, I am greater than thy Opposition that stands before me for how can I allow a uniform to stop my proceedings to lead the United States Military? These questions that take place inside of my vessel I began gathering allowing myself to start having self respect and I couldn't believe it as I stood there in front of the mirror I was the only reflection staring back at myself and than it dawned on me if I didn't stand for something I would fall for anything so I asked myself Aaron what is it that you stand for and in an amazement I received an answer and I asked myself how can one ask themselves a question and then receive an intelligent answer, as I paused to think about everything that just took place I knew it had to come from the Holy Spirit. Where God, where Yahweh, where are you? I scream for an answer back and he said if I am in an image of a man and you are a man, then I must be looking back at myself. Oh, wow father I replied what is it that you would like me to do with my time o father God? he replied stay in tuned with your lord and savior my Son Jesus. Piece together the sacrifices of the chosen ones and understand your reward is in Heaven. Remain at peace, while knowing your life has already been payed out by my son so ask yourself Aaron what shall I sacrifice for mine? Then I began to realize a man's job is to sacrifice himself to a greater mission than himself. I sat back dawned on the fact that I was consuming all, the blessings the Holy Spirit has stored inside of my life just to turn around and use them on my self. I started right there in that moment if I was going to consider my body as the vessel inside of Gods church than I need to make the right decisions with every action that I take. My second chance starts now for Yahweh has given me another day to arise, what comes with this day I have not have any idea but one thing I do know is I am, and I will be in control over my attitude, so I began to focus on my check off list to ease my mind from the stress of conquering my own dreams. Questioning myself is who makes me who I am till this day. There is not anyone that truly knows themselves until they ask themselves a question, while answering themselves with their actions of their thoughts. I can be some one, I am someone as I sit there on the stairs and cried, I have my dream, I have a family, I have my own revolving currency, but I have no home! Lost, but found, now that is a contradiction father, but it is my choice father why would I want to pay for an apartment when I can live in my car? as I pondered the next day took place and my father God Yahweh answered me!!! What, my car broke down, oh wow laughing on how the fact on how our creator speaks. He screamed out Aaron, since the beginning of time I have been relying on the foundation that I have created which relies on the foundation of Earth, one needs a home how can a King run around saving others without his own domain? yes, it must be nice to live in the free world but even than you must walk in obedience and in order to do that you must be at peace and in order to be at peace you must contain your own home, while maintaining your domain, do you understand me, Mr. Finch? yes sir, I instantly replied. From now on you shall sharpen your skills by concentrating on yourself, you shall show yourself self respect for you deserve to connect to my Kingdom here on Earth as it is in Heaven!!! For as everyone else I do to have a system that I rely on and that is why I say do not blasphemy against the Holy Spirit the creator of my son and the precious life that you endure.

HEALTH

It took me 37 years to even understand the importance of enduring life within itself let alone my health. Oh, Father God it is on and cracking you already know your boy loves a Challenge but at the same time father I cannot do it without your help, what would you like me to do? Well, remember you cannot reach me as high as you get Aaron and if you are going to smoke marijuana stop using cigars it is tobacco, the excuse of all scenarios has been eliminated when it now comes to tobacco either you are in or you are out, but do not go around lying saying you quit smoking tobacco while you are rolling up blunts made out of tobacco leaves, for my chosen leaders are never led to become Liars. To become valid in the eyes of God which is through the people I had to reconsider my approach towards life in general. What does that even mean? Well, I am glad you asked I responded my motive had to and must always be pure. Well, how do you make an unclean being clean? He said you cannot, I gave everyone a will to set them free here on Earth. healing relies on the beholder for my son has already set them free. I sat back pondering on the fact that life existed before me and life will exist after me for it is up to I to be true to myself as I display the power of God. Remember life is huge but death is even bigger for life has a time while death is for eternity!!! The steps when you are alive. Number one you will be measured by the hands of Yahweh. For one's actions holds the meaning to one's heart. Number two the way to control a man's life is through his heart. It is up to the beholder. For everyone relies on faith no matter how rich or poor, the persons measured by his or her faith for each mission on this earth takes faith to carry out Yahweh's will. Basically, telling everyone to focus on themselves allows the individual to strengthen their mental health in all situations. Causing them to become prepared in case of an event.

Patience

I learned on how to rest in the realm of the finished. For I know and I understand that everything is already done in the eyes of God but there have been many years that I have spent speaking to a psychologist, so I have been self reflecting over my mishaps in life covering every basis, so I did not repeat the same mistakes. One thing that still catches me off guard until this day is time. 86,400 seconds in a day. How do I manage while mastering time father God? With so much time it sure does fly by so fast. He told me Aaron; you are worried about the wrong area subject and topics here in life, life is about happiness, and love, focus on remaining happy. You know Father God I have never thought about it like that before, why shall I focus on only love and happiness? Then the Holy Spirit replied, Yahweh has given us the world and everything in it why care or want for anything other than love? When people display affection to one another they feel loved which makes an individual happy. I began to focus all my energy on pleasing the spirit of the next man, by paying attention to their sorrows and pain. While listening to a person's trials and tribulations it begins freeing up their spirit. By listening will give them an understanding that there are people that care, which will than open the eyes of everyone. Asking myself how can the blind lead the blind?

Yahweh no disrespect logically they cannot. That is why I send them off in pairs he said we need not to be better than the next man, but better than the previous moments. Who would want to isolate themselves forever here on earth? There must be a reason. Reasons come with the answer to one's life listen Aaron for one has two ears and one mouth why speak searching for an answer? When all you must do is sit back and listen and allow the answers to resurface. Everyone would like to be heard, and while one is courteous, the individual is more likely to relax, while telling you the truth about everything in their life. Now that is what I call communication.

Communication rules the nation Aaron. For one to understand communication one must understand Love. The connection between two individuals brings light to one's life when orchestrated right otherwise it will cause the opposite effect, which is division. So, each person must ask themselves what is it that they want from the person they encounter? After figuring this out there is only two directions this relationship can go either positive or negative. By listening to the man in front of you will allow you to notice their strengths while also figuring out their weaknesses it is up to the individual to either be respectable, guiding the person away from trouble or stay quiet and allow them to fall into the pit of hell. But ask yourself who will I blame when it is the time to be judged? This must be considered for every leader has a consequence in Heaven for leading the people astray. Why Aaron, why do you think love is an important subject when covering communication? Looking back in the mirror I honestly replied to Yahweh the energy of the next person uplifting your existence is an outstanding feeling, I have learned you treat the next person on how you would like to be treated, so in that case the feeling of love is how I reply to every person that stands in front of me for love has set me free God. Smiling back at myself screaming oh yes that was a great answer. God replied yes son it was now keep that same energy with everyone that stands before you from here on out. It is the challenges of perfection God that keeps me striving along every day for our Lords kingdom down here on earth and yet sometimes I feel like I am not carrying out everything that you need me to do. Life's lessons taught me that you look at one's heart before measured and judged, so Father God how do you read my heart? how do I instill the feeling of love to the next person? How do I walk in love without wanting anything in return I asked the Holy Spirit will you guide me? Will you teach me? Will you give me somebody to follow? Until it is my turn to lead. The Holy Spirit made me giggle in the mirror, and he said that is why he chose you. You are always worried about playing God. God is love; God just want you to focus on yourself. Aaron be happy walk in love walk in peace and allow me to be God and show you the way for the spirit is inside the vessel that your Queen has birthed, he has installed the answers to life through your lifestyle so start walking. do you know that is what my dad Charles told me he said Aaron are you not glad that you are alive then relax be at ease and know God is God. Amen father God, for I shall listen to you and my father, thank you again for the advice so that I can remain at peace through the Holy Spirit here on Earth through the spirit of your son Jesus. I thank you father for allowing me to be different than the crowds that you surrounded me around I cannot say I was bullied but I was picked on everyday by the children that were in my school for being an African American.

As I looked back at the anger that these individuals kept, it baffles my mind on how they proceeded throughout their life in a positive manner. Seeking to tear down the spirit of a young man that was lost is ludicrous. I began questioning God am I an experiment? All these white people calling me names like pick a ninny did not bother me because I did not know or understand what it meant or the history behind the evilness of the evildoers. Now of course I watched movies and read books about slavery but to see the aftermath was virtuous, to watch a race move in unity was outstanding. This is something I would love to become united with through the United States Military. "Other than death I would be in an untouchable brotherhood, surrounded by a foundation of structure. A structure that would strengthen my mind, body, spirit, and soul while guiding me in the right direction. Aaron, it is time to set a foundation before myself I spoke aloud, I have been in sports my whole life, but I am not good enough to get a full ride scholarship. I have great grades, but I do not have the funds to further my education. The time is now I will not allow anything to stop me from furthering my progressions. I am finally living out my dream, to walk with the voice of God.

I always asked people if they had all the money and power in the world here on Earth, what would they do with their time? So, when it was their time to meet God face to face and he asked them what did you do for my son's kingdom? They could reply in confidence. As I went around listening to the answers to this question made me focus on the question for myself. coming from America the melting pot made me realize that we have seven continents inside of one the entire world inside of one ideological theory placed on one plot of land. This is where my nonprofit and business

Project America limited liability corporation originated from. The ideological theory about life wrapped up in a circle implanted inside an organization for eternity underneath the sun here in America. My mission is to revise the United States Constitution while adding a Marijuana Act. Through the Marijuana Act a stimulus check will be created and will work by providing financial assistance to American citizens in 2024. The benefits of the marijuana act include providing stimulus checks to American citizens, creating opportunities for healthcare and education to be funded by the United States military, by doing this this will shed light on the monopolistic practices here in America and globally the potential drawbacks of the marijuana act could include concerns about the impact of marijuana legalization on public health, safety, and addiction rates. Additionally, there may be debates about the allocation of funds checks and potential controversies surrounding involvement of the United States, military in funding healthcare and education. These are important considerations to explore further. We can explore the implementation process of the marijuana act, including the steps involved in passing it through the legislation. The timeline for its rollout and the regulatory framework that will be established to govern the cultivation distribution and use of marijuana this is an important aspect to delve into to understand how the marijuana act will be put into practice the public can be informed about the marijuana act through various channels such as government announcements, public campaigns, media coverage, and educational outreach programs. It is important to consider how stakeholders, including the public, the public will be engaged and informed about the details, benefits, and implications of the marijuana act to ensure transparency and understanding among the population, which will then create A Second Chance Act because of the Fair Treatment Act takes place in the context of significant shifts in societal attitudes toward marijuana, which has been illegal for centuries. With its legalization, the government is now able to collect tax revenue from cannabis sales, which previously fell into the realm of illegal activities. This change highlights the need for reevaluation and reform regarding past cannabis-related offenses. The Second Chance Act aligns with this by allowing individuals with marijuana-related felony records to have their records expunged, giving them an opportunity to restart their lives without the burden of a criminal past. This act not only promotes fairness but also recognizes the need to restore dignity to those who have been affected by outdated laws. By enabling these individuals to reintegrate into society, we can foster a more inclusive environment in the United States, allowing everyone a chance to contribute positively to their communities."

In my views, a second chance act in the fair treatment act would allow the marijuana act to be able to create a stimulus check to set the veterans free that are homeless here on earth in America. These acts are lined up to create a Veteran Homeless Act here in the monopoly world inside of America. The United States military will than be able to set all American citizens free from the monopolistic practices here on earth by reuniting the principles here in life for We Stand United and United We Stand One Nation Under God. By uniting these initiatives, we are and will be working towards liberating all American citizens from oppressive practices that hinder their well-being. Together, we stand as a nation under God, committed to uplifting our veterans and ensuring that every individual could thrive in America. This coalition of acts embodies our collective responsibility to care for those who have sacrificed for our freedoms and to create a more equitable society for all."

"It is truly imperative that we give credit back to Donald J. Trump as an American citizen for opening the gates for American citizens to vote again, including those with felonies. Trump's own legal challenges, having faced 34 felonies while running for the presidency, illustrate a significant shift in the political landscape. His situation serves as a testament to the belief that redemption and second chances are vital to our nation's principles. By leading the way for those previously disenfranchised, Trump has sparked a conversation about the rights of all citizens, regardless of their past, to engage in the democratic process. This act not only empowers individuals but also reinforces the idea that every voice matters in shaping our future." This will motivate all our children here and around America to want to be apart of the movement here on Earth. To emplace in the minds of our brothers and sister faith while proving that we care here in the United States Military and that no matter what, hell or high-water we Americans will show the World that We Stand United here in America. So, the question I have for you All are you with us or Against Us? We are your brothers and sisters, moms, and dads and grandparents. This is the time to serve, stand up here in America and vote Enough, is Enough, for it is our duty to place a safety net underneath the people of today for Project America Limited liability Corporation is now in effect and will be one with the United States Military now and forever.

I ask everyone to listen up I speak to you, not as civilians on the brink of a simple decision, but as potential defenders of our great nation from the furrows of Kansas to the shores of

California, and from every walk of life and every corner of our land, hear the weight of these words enlistment is not just a contract. It is a covenant with the country. You swear to serve as you stand here, considering an oath that binds your soul to the spirit of this nation and oath that your fate with the will of the American people. The moment you etch your name on that line you become more than flesh and blood you become a sentinel of freedom An upholder of the very fabric that constitutes this union the United states constitution you have to understand this, the constitution isn't just parchment and ink it's the heart of America beating with liberty pulsing with justice it protects your rights yes, but it bestows responsibilities duties that become as essential to your being as breath itself, once you donned the uniform of this nation's military. Now let me break it down for you what it means to betray that trust. Treason, treason is a term as old as the nation itself a crime that cuts deeper than any blade. To act against your country or to side with its enemies or to harm its principles is to commit the most heinous of offenses it is to spit on the sacrifices of those who bled for our freedoms it is to turn your back on what makes us American and when you join the United States Military you commit to defend with your very life if necessary the principles laid out in the sacred document. As a soldier or a sailor, you pledged to stand against all enemies foreign and domestic and to bear true faith and allegiance to the same country you serve. Your mission, should you choose to accept it, is to embody what it means to be a unit an indomitable force forged by unity not divided by color or creed, the uniform does not care about your origins it only cares that you stand with unwavering conviction for liberty and justice for all. This is no light matter, there is no mere formality, this is about the essence of America. Today you make your choice will you rise to defend the constitution against all threats, will you commit to the ideals that bind us as a whole? Will you forsake all for the land of the free and the home of the brave? As your recruiter it is my duty to ensure you that you understand the gravity of this commitment there will be no going back there will be triumph, there might be tragedy, but above all there must be fidelity. So, I ask you now citizens standing on the precipice of greatness Are you with us fully unfalteringly unconditionally? Make your choice are you with us or against us? It is time to take your stand for in the ranks of America's military there is no room for half hearted allegiances there is only the full measure of devotion to the United States of America and its constitution God be with you for the path is noble and the burden eternal.

System VS. The People

What does the American people even mean to our government? If America is not over our own currency? Who is? If resources of the land rule the nation what resources is America lacking to put America into poverty? 7 continents have their own individual military units with at least 1 ruler over each military personnel. So, who is over the Sovereign King? What individual is not affected by the laws of the land? And why? We are willing to put our lives on the line for our country. Would you agree that our country should be over our own currency system and if not, that should be the area we should be facing when it comes to war. As citizens we all need to pause and come to a standstill. Enough is enough Project America Incorporated will be the new beginning for our generations to come, for America should never be dictated by another leader in another country for the American Citizens need to be in charge over our own decisions here in America. For it takes us all as one to become whole and that is the terms United We Stand. America's ideological theory about showing the rest of the nations that all races can come together has already taken place. We as the people need to stand together about our currency issues for America's government and military should have infinity and beyond dollars. The United States

Military holds while protecting the creation of the dollar bill for this country. Who our we serving? And why? For this is the Land of the Free so it is time to set us all free from humility and self-gather our dignity for were all human beings and were all equal, so it is time to stand together this will set us all free back to the Promise Land. There is not anything wrong with a system, but it takes a human to run and follow one not only does it take one to use it. It takes a human to create one leaving the fact that a system needs a human to help operate it. This would be the start of a new beginning for America, to be able to keep the system by strengthening the foundations here in our own backyard. By inspiring people to focus their next steps in life, will grasp our children's attention. Allowing the government to Recruit more soldiers and sailors. Allowing a choice here in life to either get down with the red, white, and blue and be free here in this world or fend for your own. By keeping our children in shape, they will be able to enlist for at least 4 years in the military. Opening avenues for our citizens will strengthen our military. Brothers and sisters by inventing a way to keep the people positive and occupied lessons crimes. This helps individuals watch each other, creating new structures for our government.

Changing people's perspective on you in a community where you are seen as a nuisance can be a challenging task, but it is possible with effort and determination. Here are some steps you can take to improve how others perceive you: 1. Reflect on your behavior: Take a step back and honestly evaluate your actions and how they may have contributed to the negative perception of you. This will help you identify any patterns or behaviors that may be causing friction with others. 2. Apologize and make amends: If you have wronged or offended anyone in the community, apologize sincerely and make amends to show that you are willing to take responsibility for your actions. 3. Show respect and kindness: Treat others in the community with respect and kindness, even if they have not treated you well in the past. Be polite, considerate, and willing to listen to others' perspectives. 4. Get involved in community activities: Show that you are committed to being a positive member of the community by getting involved in community activities, volunteering, or participating in any local events. This can help you build connections and show that you are invested in the well-being of the community. 5. Seek feedback and make changes: Ask for feedback from others in the community on how you can improve and make changes based on their suggestions. Demonstrating a willingness to learn and grow can help change people's perceptions of you. 6. Be patient and persistent: Changing people's perceptions takes time, so be patient and persistent in your efforts to improve how others see you. Consistently demonstrating positive behavior and making an effort to connect with others can help rebuild trust and change people's opinions of you over time. Remember that changing people's perspectives on you may not happen overnight, but with consistent effort and a genuine desire to improve, you can make a positive impact and rebuild your reputation in the community.

The blessing of sight is a blessing as the next generation it is important for us to grasp all reality that takes place here on earth and inside America. For it is up to us as the next generation to further advance our society and keep the principals of our constitution over our citizens here in America. While being raised by our elders we for see a lot of their decisions that they make due to their feeling and as a community we must figure out the importance of our citizens in our society. Majority of us citizens must partake in some type of labor to maintain a healthy balance in our life style due to the bills needing to be paid, food and shelter and as a child to our adult hood we see our elders partaking in this structure letting us know that we cannot survive in this world without some type of employment. So, we need to come to some type of an agreement and create a safety net for our elders here in America for there is one thing you cannot cheat and that is time. From 16 to 55 years old is 39 years of employment here in America giving our time and energy to the labor structure in life for life is also a blessing in itself. How one is determined to work so that he or she can have some sort of a balanced life is another story but with our free-will we need to determine that a senior citizen cannot and will not be homeless here in America by creating a Senior Citizen Homeless Act and a Senior Citizen Disability Homeless Act for our elders 55 years of age and older. While creating a Veteran Homeless Act, for we the people say enough is enough and that our Elders and Veterans should not Suffer.

The Marijuana Act

Project America envisions using strategically placed personnel to watch and infiltrate illicit drug networks, thereby ensuring that the legalization of marijuana does not inadvertently support illegal drug trade activities. By embedding spies within various sectors, including the military, agricultural, and business communities, the project looks to gather critical intelligence.

These operatives will work closely with domestic law enforcement and international allies to trace the origins and pathways of illegal substances entering the United States. With support from the United States military and other federal agencies, Project America intends to dismantle these networks, effectively safeguard national security, and uphold the integrity of legal markets.

The collaboration with Project America LLC, adds a layer of private sector agility to this initiative, allowing for innovative approaches and rapid deployment of resources. This partnership emphasizes a unified effort under the tenets of respect, shared mission, and legal compliance, reflecting the project's core values and dedication to the country's defense.

By assembling a diverse team of operatives who align with both national defense goals and individual ethical beliefs, Project America aspires to not only protect citizens but also contribute positively to a just and lawful society.

"The United States military, with its extensive logistical capabilities and organizational strength, will act as the backbone for this ambitious initiative. By overseeing the distribution and management of the financial resources generated by the marijuana act, they ensure a dependable monthly stimulus check reaches every American citizen. This unprecedented move aims not only at economic stability but also at granting social freedom and security for future generations.

By using profits from the regulated cannabis industry, these funds provide a safety net, forming the cornerstone of an economic model that promises to uplift all citizens. This constructive collaboration between national defense and domestic welfare sets a new standard for how governmental institutions can cooperate to foster prosperity.

The broader vision entails employing innovative technology and robust frameworks to safeguard the integrity and continuity of this system. This way, citizens are afforded not just financial relief, but a guarantee of long-term economic freedom throughout their lives, embodying the true spirit of liberty and justice for all." This initiative not only honors the sacrifices of our veterans by granting them meaningful employment but also ensures their comfortable reintegration into society. By covering essential living expenses through a basic allowance for housing, these veterans can focus on their duties without the stress of financial burdens. They step into the free world, standing proudly beneath the red, white, and blue of the United States American flag, with a renewed sense of purpose and belonging. This alignment with national symbols underlines a commitment to unity and empowerment, as we collectively move towards a future where freedom and service go hand in hand. In conclusion, unity is provided by the United States military, a structure honored by human beings loved by our country. Marijuana brings peace to this earth which calms down the people here in America. Let us give a second chance for American citizens to structure themselves financially so that the American citizens do not get demolished by the financial structure of this world.

Exploring the impact of marijuana legalization reveals both promising opportunities and challenges. Economically, the legalization has opened doors to a burgeoning industry that boosts job creation and generates substantial tax revenue.

This economic boon has provided funds for public services and infrastructure, enhancing community development.

Furthermore, legalization has prompted a reevaluation of criminal justice policies, leading to reduced incarceration rates for non-violent drug offenses. This shift not only alleviates the strain on correctional facilities but also allows individuals previously marginalized by drug-related charges to reintegrate into society with dignity.

However, challenges are still, till this day. Regulation of marijuana is still complex, requiring the careful balancing of public health concerns and market dynamics. Education on responsible consumption is necessary to prevent potential misuse, especially among younger generations. Moreover, federal policies lag state-level innovations, causing a unified framework to harmonize regulations across jurisdictions.

Ultimately, the journey toward widespread marijuana legalization reflects a broader societal quest for justice, health, and prosperity. As this movement gains momentum, it holds the potential to reshape societal norms and foster more fair economic structures for future generations. Within this structured support system, religious objectors can engage in agricultural projects, helping to supply food and resources both domestically and internationally. This allows them to fulfill their duty in a manner that aligns with their convictions, fostering a sense of purpose and duty without compromising their beliefs.

Project America LLC will act as a bridge between these individuals and the military's mission, ensuring that religious convictions are respected while still contributing to a robust national security framework. As we look to the future, this model could present potential challenges, such as integrating these roles within traditional military operations. However, the predicted benefits, including enhanced morale and diversified contributions to national objectives, are vast.

By focusing on this symbiotic relationship, we can ensure that every service member, regardless of their religious stance, has a place and a purpose that honors their beliefs and supports global and national efforts.

Project America's main goal is to support the United States military by fostering an environment where free will, mission purpose, and respectful communication are emphasized. It aims to create a space where individuals who may have objections to traditional military service can still contribute meaningfully and respectfully to the nation's defense efforts, without compromising their personal beliefs or values.

The Fair Treatment Act aims to provide direct support to families affected by marijuana-related incarcerations and broader societal challenges, offering several targeted benefits:

1. **Financial Assistance: ** Through stimulus checks and limited financial support, families can manage essential expenses such as housing, food, healthcare, and education. This helps alleviate immediate financial pressures that may have been exacerbated by the incarceration of a family member.

2. **Reintegration Programs: ** These programs will aid in smoothly transitioning formerly incarcerated individuals back into their families and communities, offering job training and employment opportunities that enhance long-term family stability.

3. **Emotional and Psychological Support: ** Access to counseling and family therapy can aid in healing relationships strained by separation, supporting the mental well-being of both parents and children.

4. **Educational Opportunities: ** Providing scholarships and educational grants can help children from affected families pursue academic goals, breaking cycles of

disadvantage and opening pathways to college and career success.

5. **Community and Social Services Access: ** The Act could bolster local support systems, ensuring families have access to needed social services like childcare, healthcare, and community-building activities, fostering a supportive environment for rebuilding family unity.

By addressing these areas, the Fair Treatment Act looks to offer comprehensive support to families, helping them rebuild and thrive. If there are other ways you would like to see the Act supporting families, or if you have specific areas of interest, feel free to let me know! My email address is Hollywoodg420@gmail.com.

By setting up a "safety net," Project America encourages participation from a diverse range of individuals, promoting respect and understanding while aligning with the overarching mission of protecting and serving the country. The Silver Back Gorillaz Secret Service Agents are composed of highly skilled individual assassins trained by the Navy Seals that undertakes covert operations aimed at disrupting illegal activities involving alcohol, tobacco, firearms, and now marijuana. This elite group runs with precision and stealth to ensure the enforcement of laws across the United States, using their unique training and skills.

The formation of this unit was prompted by a significant rise in organized crime and smuggling activities that threatened national security. By integrating specialists with combat expertise and in-depth knowledge of the underworld networks, the Navy seeks to bring about a swift and effective response to these growing problems.

With the inclusion of marijuana as a focus area, the unit is tasked with navigating the complex and evolving legal landscape, ensuring that the new policies are adhered to while respecting states' rights and federal mandates. They face challenges from both the criminal elements looking to exploit grey areas in the law and political figures who question the militarization of domestic law enforcement.

Despite these obstacles, their mission remains clear: to uphold justice and public safety by dismantling sophisticated criminal operations, one mission at a time while "Placing a Safety Net Underneath the people of Today. This bold and unprecedented measure, championed by the United States military monopoly act, promises to redefine the socio-economic landscape for generations to come. By leveraging the resources and authority vested in the military, the act aims not only to regulate the marijuana industry but also to channel the massive economic inflows directly into the hands of every American citizen.

The initiative seeks to establish a perpetual stimulus check system, ensuring a basic income floor that empowers individuals across all socioeconomic backgrounds. This move is expected to revolutionize how citizens engage with the economy, providing them with unprecedented financial security and stability.

By establishing a marijuana act, soldiers and sailors will have the opportunity to unite around an agriculture program. This initiative not only provides them with a tangible mission but cultivates a sense of purpose and connection to the land they defend. It instills pride and responsibility to uphold the core values embodied in the red, white, and blue—the United States Constitution—and motivates them to champion human humanity on Earth.

Such a program could focus on sustainable cultivation practices, promoting environmental stewardship while contributing to local economies. The skills developed within this agricultural framework could be invaluable for their personal growth and post-service careers, offering a new avenue for veterans to integrate into civilian life effectively.

Furthermore, this act could facilitate cross-cultural exchanges and foster diplomatic ties using agricultural knowledge to aid other nations, strengthening global communities and support systems. By championing a cause that aligns with both constitutional values and global humanitarian goals, the U.S. military could find renewed inspiration and a unified mission to guide its operations both domestically and internationally.

Such a visionary plan is set to bolster not only individual welfare but also stimulate broader economic growth, spurring innovation, entrepreneurship, and community development. In addition to the obvious financial advantages, this act has the potential to foster a healthier society by addressing long-standing inequalities and social disparities Through thoughtful collaboration and strategic implementation, the United States stands to become a beacon of progressive policy and inclusive prosperity on the global stage so welcome to America, the land of the free, where opportunities are limitless and the spirit of innovation thrives. Our nation is built on the principles of liberty and justice for all, creating an environment where everyone has the chance to chase their aspirations. Here, diversity and unity go hand in hand, embodying the true essence of the American dream. This is a place where voices are heard, and every individual has the right to take part in shaping the future. Join us in celebrating the values of freedom, equality, and the land of opportunity. God bless America and welcome to Heaven here on Earth by yours truly King Aaron Michael Finch.

www.ingramcontent.com/pod-product-compliance
Lightning Source LLC
Chambersburg PA
CBHW061319250726

48653CB00002B/966